W9-BHR-944

NASHVILLE PUBLIC LIBRARY

FOUNDATION

This book given
to the Nashville Public Library
through the generosity of the
**Dollar General
Literacy Foundation**

NPLF.ORG

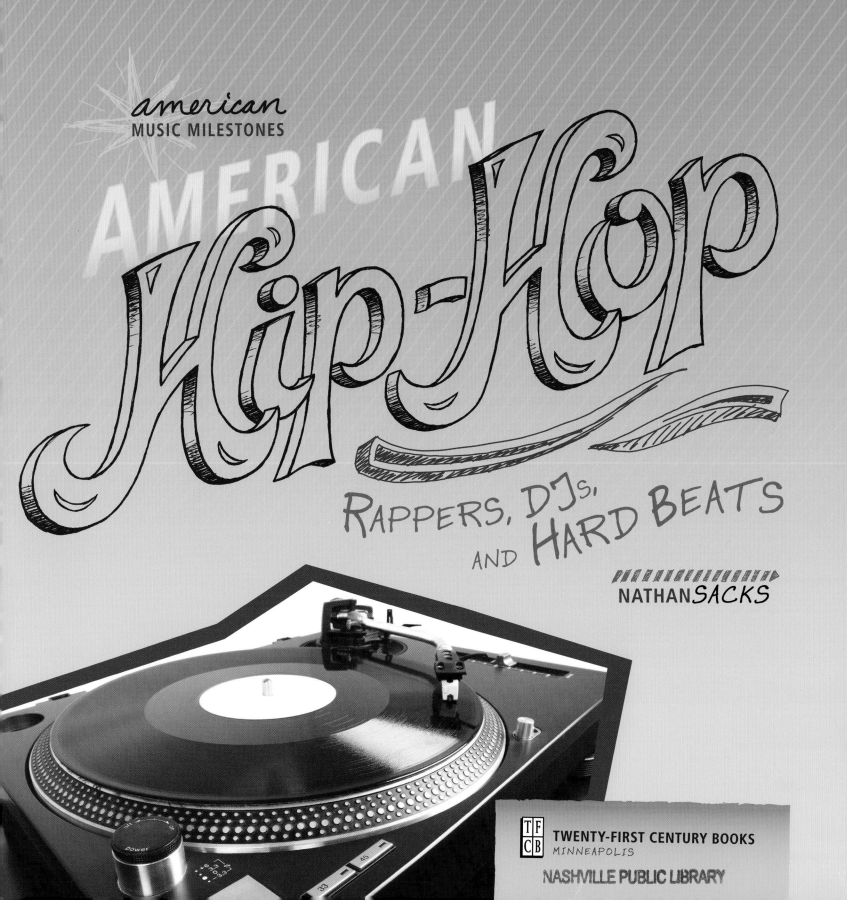

american
MUSIC MILESTONES

AMERICAN Hip-Hop

RAPPERS, DJs, AND HARD BEATS

NATHAN SACKS

TFCB TWENTY-FIRST CENTURY BOOKS
MINNEAPOLIS

NASHVILLE PUBLIC LIBRARY

NOTE TO READERS: some songs and music videos by artists discussed in this book contain language and images that readers may consider offensive.

Copyright © 2013 by Nathan Sacks

All rights reserved. International copyright secured. No part of this book may be reproduced, stored in a retrieval system, or transmitted in any form or by any means—electronic, mechanical, photocopying, recording, or otherwise—without the prior written permission of Lerner Publishing Group, Inc., except for the inclusion of brief quotations in an acknowledged review.

Twenty-First Century Books
A division of Lerner Publishing Group, Inc.
241 First Avenue North
Minneapolis, MN 55401 U.S.A.

Website address: www.lernerbooks.com

Library of Congress Cataloging-in-Publication Data

Sacks, Nathan.
    American hip-hop: Rappers, DJs, and Hard Beats / by Nathan Sacks.
      p.   cm. — (American music milestones)
    Includes bibliographical references and index.
    ISBN: 978–0–7613–4500–8 (lib. bdg. : alk. paper)
    1. Rap (Music)—History and criticism—Juvenile literature. I. Title.
  ML3531.S23 2013
  782.42164909—dc23   2011045580

Manufactured in the United States of America
1 – CG – 7/15/12

CONTENTS

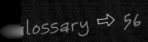

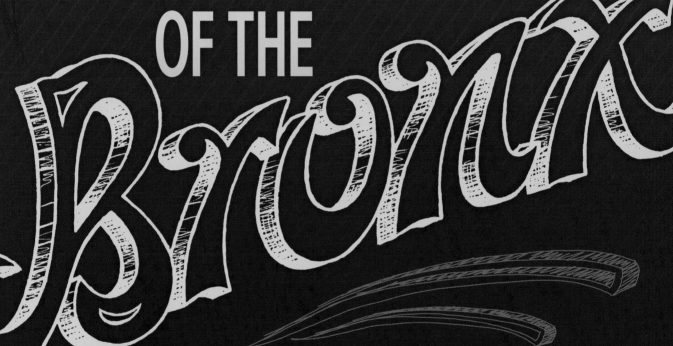

chapter 1

BUSTING OUT
OF THE
Bronx

IN 1978 A FIFTEEN-MINUTE TRACK CALLED "RAPPER'S DELIGHT" INTRODUCED THE WORLD TO A NEW SOUND.

The song's beat came from a popular dance tune, but the vocals were something else. Instead of singing, members of the Sugarhill Gang "rapped" to the beat. The Sugarhill Gang was not the first group to combine funk and dance music with rhythmic spoken rhymes, but it was one of the first groups to score a hit with that style of music. The song marked the beginning of a revolution.

When hip-hop first hit the scene, its sounds were meant for clubs and dance floors. Even after "Rapper's Delight" became a hit, not many people took the music seriously. Mainstream radio and the cable channel MTV rejected it. But over time, hip-hop became a multibillion-dollar business that dominates the airwaves and a respected art form.

Twenty-first-century rappers such as Lil Wayne, Kanye West, and Drake are some of the world's biggest celebrities. These artists play sold-out stadium shows and have millions of fans. Some are also praised as powerful lyricists and songwriters. But it took a long time for hip-hop to reach that level of respect.

Hip-hop's journey started even before "Rapper's Delight." The history of the music begins in the Bronx, a borough (district) of New York City. One of the poorest and most racially divided areas in the country, the Bronx was where a group of DJs (disc jockeys) forged the sound that changed music forever.

RIGHT: The Sugarhill Gang scored one of hip-hop's earliest hits with "Rapper's Delight" (1978).

BOTTOM: The New York City borough known as the Bronx was home to pioneering hip-hop performers such as DJ Kool Herc and Grandmaster Flash.

A B-boy lets loose in New York City's Washington Square Park in the early 1980s. B-boys, or break boys, added wild dance moves to hip-hop culture.

RAP AND
HIP-HOP

Although rap is a crucial part of hip-hop, the two terms do not mean the same thing. Rapping is the act of speaking rhyming lyrics, often over instrumental music. People from different cultures had rapped prior to the birth of hip-hop. Storytellers in western Africa spoke their tales in rhyme centuries before Jay-Z picked up a mic. African Americans living under slavery also included spoken-word rhymes in the spirituals (religious songs) they sang. By the early 1970s, American poets such as Gil Scott-Heron made delivering words out loud a part of their art form.

Hip-hop music combines rapped lyrics with instrumental music. Sometimes this music is taken from other songs. Sometimes it is played live or created in a recording studio. As hip-hop music grew in popularity, a whole culture grew around it. Hip-hop became a group of traditions, styles, and attitudes.

According to the DJ Afrika Bambaataa, hip-hop culture has four main elements. One element is called breaking. The earliest hip-hop songs took their beats from disco music. Disco was a type of dance music that became popular in clubs during the 1970s. Many disco songs had instrumental breaks.

Graffiti covers this wall in New York City's Harlem neighborhood, pictured here in 1991. New York's first hip-hop generation turned "tagging" the walls of local buildings into an art form.

During a break, the singer stops and lets the song's beats take over.

For dance crews at the clubs, breaks were the time to show off their moves. These dancers were called B-boys, or break boys. Being a B-boy meant knowing a lot of hard tricks, such as somersaults and handstand poses. Dancing like this took a lot of energy and practice. It could also be dangerous. A lot of bones would be broken from break dance routines gone amok.

Tagging is another element of hip-hop. In the Bronx of the 1970s, many young African Americans became involved in gangs, or "crews." Artists in these crews used bottles of spray paint to make gang art. They would spray, or "tag," their crew's logo on buildings, in alleys, and under bridges. This was a way of marking territory. Though tagging was illegal, these artists added more color to struggling neighborhoods.

DJs invented two of hip-hop music's signature sounds: scratching (spinning a record against a turntable needle) and sampling (taking a section from one song and putting it in another song).

DJing and emceeing are the other two elements of hip-hop. Disc jockeys make beats and spin records during performances. In the early days of hip-hop, that meant playing records on a turntable. Over time, DJs turned the record player into an instrument of its own. They did this by scratching, or spinning a record against the turntable needle. By scratching, DJs could move back and forth between instrumental breaks. They could play one part of a song over and over. DJs also helped pioneer sampling. They took part of a recording from one song and put it in another. People who collect samples and put them together in the studio are usually called producers.

The heart of hip-hop culture is emceeing, or rapping. Emcee is another way of writing "MC." The abbreviation means "master of ceremonies"—the guy or girl who runs the show. Like breaking, tagging, and DJing, emceeing developed into its own art. MCs, or rappers, were judged by their flow, or their ability to spit (deliver) lyrical rhymes. The first rappers were inspired by the vocals they heard in funk music and spoken-word poetry. Later rappers became known for their ability to freestyle, to come up with rhymes as they are rapping.

HIP-HOP SAMPLE SUPERSTARS

Soul singer **James Brown** (TOP) is probably the most sampled artist in hip-hop history. His drummers' tight grooves were made for rapping over. Brown's 1970 song "Funky Drummer" may be his most sampled song because of drummer Clyde Stubblefield's famous beat. Among the few artists who can challenge James Brown for the title of "most sampled" is funk king **George Clinton** (BOTTOM). Many rappers have rhymed over Clinton's 1982 song "Atomic Dog." Clinton has also worked directly with rap artists such as OutKast and the Wu-Tang Clan.

However, not all samples are taken from popular artists. In fact, some of the most used samples come from little-known songs. The funk artist Melvin Bliss is better known for the grooves of "Synthetic Substitution" (1973) than for anything else he ever wrote.

Most rappers write down lyrics before they perform. But gifted freestylers create rhymes off the top of their head.

In addition to its four basic elements, hip-hop is also about fashion, politics, and the state of inner-city America. The rapper Chuck D once called hip-hop the "black CNN." He meant that hip-hop covers the urban black experience in ways that mainstream news sources often ignore. Throughout hip-hop history, rappers have kept coming back to the same themes: poverty, drug addiction, joblessness, single motherhood, and rage at racial discrimination and injustice. Many, though not all, hip-hop lyrics include graphic language. Rappers use street slang, swear words, and explicit sexual terms to depict the realities of their lives.

Kool Herc spins records at a 2006 party in New York City. Herc threw his first party—a hip-hop landmark—in 1973.

KOOL HERC

Hip-hop culture begins with the sound. And the sound was first heard in an apartment complex on 1520 Sedgwick Avenue in the East Bronx. Before arriving in New York City, Clive Campbell was a kid living in the island nation of Jamaica. He loved R & B (rhythm and blues) and dancehall music. In 1967, when he was twelve, he moved with his mother to the United States. Campbell's love for music led him to some local dance clubs. There he joined

[DJ Kool] Herc wasn't like a rapper or anything like that; it was just a sound, his music, his system. The music that he played was just like no other.

—Sha-Rock of the hip-hop group the Funky Four Plus One, 2002

his first graffiti crew, the Ex-Vandals. As an Ex-Vandal, Campbell learned tagging and breaking.

Clive wanted to play his own music, so he invited some friends to a party. He wrote the name "Kool Herc" on an invitation sent around the neighborhood. On August 11, 1973, he gave his first show on Sedgwick Avenue. The show was a massive success. From then on, he started hosting regular parties. Clive Campbell became known as DJ Kool Herc. August 11, 1973, is known as the day hip-hop was born.

Herc's shows became popular all over the South Bronx. He would play classic soul and R & B artists such as the Isley Brothers, Aretha Franklin, and James Brown. At that time, it was rare to hear those artists on the radio. Eventually, Kool Herc formed his own hip-hop crew, the Herculoids. He also started building a louder sound system to keep up with the growing crowds.

With the help of his Herculoids, DJ Kool Herc crafted the style of early hip-hop. First, he learned how to repeat a break. Herc found that many instrumental grooves (rhythmic musical parts) were too short. Some breaks were only a couple

Legends, FROM LEFT TO RIGHT: Grandmaster Flash, Kool Herc, Afrika Bambaataa, and Chuck D of Public Enemy BOTTOM, gathered together for Columbia University's Rap Summit in 1993.

seconds long, but they were the parts of songs that dancers liked the most. Herc repeated grooves by switching between copies of the same record on two different turntables. By repeating the beat, B-boys and B-girls could dance as long as they wanted.

While Herc was developing his DJ style, his friend Coke La Rock decided to try rhyming words on Herc's microphone. La Rock's rhymes were simple at first. He boasted and rapped messages to friends. Soon others tried stepping to the mic as well. Herc himself would even rhyme on occasion. Rapping over the music became part of the show.

Before long, Herc's sound was piping out of every Bronx street corner. Unlike the DJs who followed, Herc never recorded a single or an album. It would be up to the next wave to bring hip-hop to the radio.

GETTING FURIOUS

Along with DJ Kool Herc, Grandmaster Flash helped define the early years of hip-hop. He helped make hip-hop popular by producing original music with his own crew. Like Herc, Grandmaster Flash was born in another country, Barbados. He came to the South Bronx as a young child. Flash (Joseph Saddler)

Grandmaster Flash, seen here in the early 1980s, made hip-hop with a message. The members of Flash's crew the Furious Five rapped about the hardships of urban life.

MORE of the OLD SCHOOL

...master Flash, DJ Kool Herc, and Afrika Bambaataa
...t the only artists who added to the hip-hop movement.
...Blow (ABOVE) became the first rapper to sign to a major
...th the song "Christmas Rappin'" (1979). Kool Moe Dee
... of the first and best freestyle rappers. And of course,
...arhill Gang broke the music into the mainstream with
...mous fifteen-minute dance track "Rapper's Delight."

was obsessed with listening to records, even from a young age. He loved his father's record collection so much that he was inspired to build his own speakers.

Flash was impressed by the massive sound system at Herc's parties. He created a system through which he could listen to breaks with headphones shortly before playing them live. This way, he knew what part of a song was coming next before his listeners did. Flash also added to Herc's style by making "scratching" part of the rhythm of a song. With record players of the time, DJs scratched by moving the record against the turntable needle. Flash used the record needle as an instrument to add a "whooshing" sound to tracks.

In the mid-1970s, Grandmaster Flash and lead MC Melle Mel formed the Furious Five—the first important group in hip-hop history. In 1982 the Five released the single "The Message." It was one of the first rap songs to describe the poor conditions of black neighborhoods. The album *The Message* (1982) had the song "White Lines," which warned about the dangers of cocaine use. It became an influence for "conscious" hip-hop. In conscious hip-hop, the lyrics focus on the struggles of African Americans and minorities. In contrast, party raps focus on getting people dancing.

OUT OF THIS WORLD

Afrika Bambaataa (Kevin Donovan), also from the Bronx, was inspired by DJ Kool Herc's style too. But he took the music in a different direction. While Herc stuck to disco and soul, Afrika Bambaataa brought diversity to hip-hop. Bambaataa loved rock bands such as the Rolling Stones as much as he loved James Brown. Inspired by a trip to Africa, Bambaataa formed a crew called the Universal Zulu Nation and started DJing at parties. He hoped to use the Nation and its music to get young people away from crime and drugs.

Afrika Bambaataa brought new sounds to hip-hop music. His club hit "Planet Rock" (1982) even sampled German techno music.

Bambaataa had a club hit in 1982 with the single "Planet Rock." The song combined hip-hop and techno music. Instead of sampling from American dance or soul records, Bambaataa took the melody from a German electronic band called Kraftwerk. Afrika Bambaataa is therefore known as a pioneer of electronic music as well as hip-hop. ★

MUST DOWNLOAD Playlist

GIL SCOTT-HERON
"The Bottle" (1974)

THE SUGARHILL GANG
"Rapper's Delight (12" version)" (1978)

LADY B
"To the Beat, Y'all" (1979)

SPOONIE GEE
"Spoonin' Rap" (1979)

FUNKY FOUR PLUS ONE
"That's the Joint" (1980)

GRAND WIZZARD THEODORE AND THE FANTASTIC FIVE
"Can I Get a Soul Clap" (1980)

KURTIS BLOW
"The Breaks" (1980)

TREACHEROUS THREE
"The New Rap Language" (1980)

AFRIKA BAMBAATAA
"Planet Rock" (1982)

GRANDMASTER FLASH AND THE FURIOUS FIVE
"The Message" (1982)

Chapter 2

OLD SCHOOL TO New School

Debbie Harry, singer of the white pop band Blondie, hangs out on the set of the "Rapture" music video. Harry spits a rap verse on the song "Rapture" (1980).

BY THE EARLY 1980s, HIP-HOP MUSIC WAS NO LONGER JUST A BRONX THING.

It had reached New York City's other boroughs. Early rappers such as Kurtis Blow and Fab Five Freddy were becoming local celebrities. The record industry began to take notice. But hip-hop still had a long way to go before it would be accepted by the mainstream.

In the early 1980s, many mainstream radio stations refused to play hip-hop music. They saw hip-hop as a passing craze. Or they believed it was not real "music," because it borrowed sounds from other songs. Others believed its lyrics—often laced with swearing and sexual imagery—were offensive. Still others felt the music had no appeal for white listeners. MTV launched in 1981, but the channel ignored music by African Americans until pop singer Michael Jackson broke through with his video for the song "Billie Jean" in 1983. It would still be a few years until a rap group video was played on MTV.

Critics who claimed that hip-hop worked only for black audiences were not paying attention. The white pop band Blondie released a single called "Rapture" in 1981. It had a funky hip-hop beat and a rap verse from singer Debbie Harry. The dance tune "Genius of Love" (1981), by the Tom Tom Club, was another mainstream radio hit inspired by hip-hop. In that song, singer-bassist Tina Weymouth

The pop and R & B singer Michael Jackson was one of the first African-American artists to be played on MTV. The video for Jackson's 1983 song "Billie Jean" paved the way for other black performers.

> I see hip-hop culture as the new American mainstream. We don't change for you; you adapt to us.
>
> —Russell Simmons, Def Jam cofounder, 2001

Russell Simmons in the recording studio in 1993. Simmons, a hip-hop businessperson, helped groups such as Run-D.M.C. reach wide audiences.

mentions Kurtis Blow by name. Hip-hop's new fans understood that the message was meant for everyone.

THE NEW KINGS OF RAP

Hip-hop culture would shift once again as the era of "old school" rap gave way to the "new school." Russell Simmons led the charge. Simmons was a hip-hop promoter who organized concerts and advertised artists in the late 1970s. He managed Kurtis Blow and helped produce "Christmas Rappin'." When Blow needed a DJ, Russell recommended his brother Joseph Simmons. Onstage, Joseph became known as DJ Run. Soon he was rapping on the mic alongside Blow.

Inspired to start his own group, Joseph asked his friend Darryl McDaniels to join him. Russell hooked up the duo with DJ Jason Mizell. McDaniels called himself D.M.C., while Mizell became Jam Master Jay. Meanwhile, Russell Simmons and the white producer Rick Rubin formed the Def Jam music label. In 1983 Run-D.M.C. released its first single, "It's Like That," on Def Jam Records. With the help of Simmons's promotion, "It's Like That" was a successful debut.

The hip-hop group Run-D.M.C. formed in Queens, New York. Working with producer Rick Rubin, Run-D.M.C. transformed hip-hop with its tough but radio-friendly sound. They are pictured here in 1986.

Run-D.M.C.'s new school sound was different from the old school's disco and funk samples. The group's members rapped over the robotic rhythms of drum machines. Like Afrika Bambaataa, they believed that hip-hop songs could sample anything. They especially liked hard rock music. Their second album, **King of Rock** (1985), was a tribute to that genre. The group's fusion of hip-hop beats and metal guitar riffs became very popular.

Run-D.M.C.'s third album **Raising Hell** (1986) broke the group to a mainstream audience. That album included "My Adidas," a tribute to sneakers. The song helped the group sign an endorsement deal with Adidas. This was the first time a rap group officially advertised a corporate product. Another track, "Walk This Way," sampled a hit song from the rock group Aerosmith. Aerosmith members Steven Tyler and Joe Perry liked Run-D.M.C.'s version. They appeared in the song's music video. As a result, "Walk This Way" was the first rap video to receive major MTV airplay.

Run-D.M.C. became the first global hip-hop group. In 1985 it was the only rap act invited to perform at Live Aid in Philadelphia, Pennsylvania. Live Aid was a global charity concert that aimed to end world hunger. Millions of people watched the concert on TV. Run-D.M.C.'s performance introduced hip-hop to many music fans from other countries. But the new school sound didn't stay at the top of the hip-hop world forever.

"THREE IDIOTS"

In the early 1980s, many white teenagers heard hip-hop for the first time. One hardcore punk (extremely fast, aggressive rock) band was especially inspired by the music. Mike D (Mike Diamond), MCA (Adam Yauch), and Ad-Rock (Adam Horovitz) were three Jewish kids who had been playing in New York's punk scene. They called themselves the Beastie Boys.

As a joke, the Beasties released a hip-hop single called "Cooky Puss" in 1982. That song inspired the group to make a complete switch from punk to hip-hop. They hooked up with Simmons and Rubin and signed to Def Jam. Not many people expected the Beastie Boys to succeed. They were white and not very impressive rappers.

The Beastie Boys shocked the world when the album **Licensed to Ill** (1986) turned out to be a huge hit. New York's **Village Voice** magazine printed the headline "Three Idiots Make a Masterpiece." Critics and rap fans called it one of the best albums ever. Like Run-D.M.C., the Beastie Boys used rock guitars in their beats. Heavy songs such as "Fight for Your Right (to Party)" became rap standards. The Beastie Boys were the first white rap group to make it in the industry.

The Beastie Boys, performing here in 1987, have changed musical styles many times. Before giving hip-hop a try, the group even played punk rock.

THE ORIGINAL FEMALE MCs

The first rap single ever, "Rapper's Delight" (1979), was produced by a woman. Sylvia Robinson (TOP) was already a singer and songwriter, but her detour into hip-hop changed music forever. Although Robinson didn't rap on the song herself, she oversaw its release. Robinson later encouraged Grandmaster Flash and his crew to record "The Message" (1982).

Sha-Rock (MIDDLE) was one of the first female emcees. She was part of the group Funky Four Plus One. The success of their song "That's the Joint" (1980) led to an early appearance on TV's *Saturday Night Live*. MC Lyte (BOTTOM) and the group Salt-N-Pepa followed Sha-Rock's lead. MC Lyte became the first female to release a solo rap album in 1988. *Lyte as a Rock* challenged the male dominance of hip-hop. Cheryl "Salt" James, Sandy "Pepa" Denton, and Deidre "Spinderella" Roper were like a female version of Run-D.M.C. Their hit song "Push It" (1986) became a radio classic of the late 1980s.

Most rap acts have short lives, but the Beastie Boys have been a group for almost thirty years. Their second album *Paul's Boutique* (1989) used samples with surprising artistry. It was the first sign that the group was becoming more mature. Over the decades, the Beasties have focused on more social and political issues. In 1996 they helped organize concerts that protested China's presence in the Asian region of Tibet. The Beastie Boys are also known for their striking, humorous music videos. The group released its eighth album, *Hot Sauce Committee Part Two*, in 2011.

LADIES LOVE
COOL
JAMES

James Smith was another Queens (New York) resident who worshipped hip-hop culture from an early age. At the time he broke through, he was one of the youngest rappers in the game. Like the Beastie Boys, he signed to Def Jam.

LL Cool J burst onto the hip-hop scene with the song "I Can't Live Without My Radio" (1985). His clever raps charmed female fans and impressed fellow emcees.

Smith called himself LL Cool J, or "Ladies Love Cool James." His first popular record was "I Can't Live Without My Radio" in 1985.

As a rapper, LL Cool J is known mostly for two things. The first is his skill with battle rhymes. Battle rhyming is a style in which rappers take turns dissing (or disrespecting) one another in rap form. Accompanied by the drum machines and hard guitars for which Def Jam was known, LL Cool J hurled clever insults at his rivals in songs such as "Mama Said Knock You Out." Secondly, LL was one of the first rappers to make smooth, romantic hip-hop aimed at women. Such songs as "I Need Love" showed the more sensitive side of a rapper known mostly for his boasts. By working in two styles, LL Cool J showed that a rapper can have many different sides to his personality.

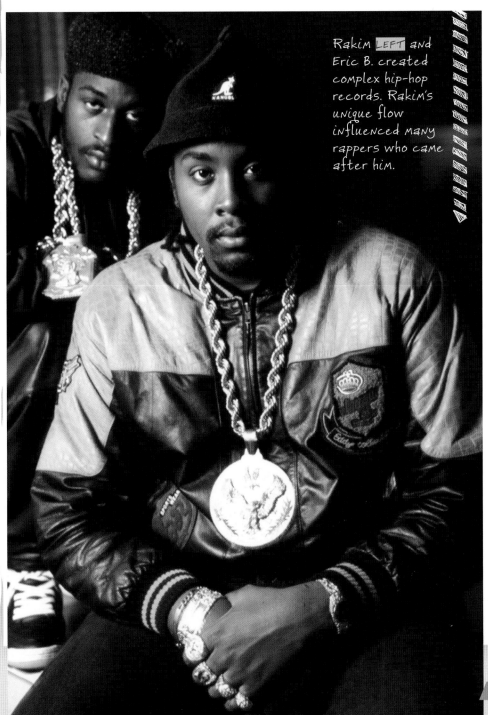

Rakim LEFT and Eric B. created complex hip-hop records. Rakim's unique flow influenced many rappers who came after him.

GOD ON THE MIC: ERIC B. AND RAKIM

Before Rakim (William Griffin Jr.), rappers followed a simple formula. Raps were divided into bars, or one line of a verse. Most rappers would rhyme the last words of a pair of bars and then move on to a new rhyme. In 1987 Rakim and his DJ Eric B. changed that. Rakim's rhymes didn't follow the usual patterns.

On songs from the duo's first album, *Paid in Full* (1987), Rakim rhymed the same word several times within the span of a bar. This style is called internal rhyming. For instance, on the song "I Ain't

No Joke," Rakim rhymes "joke" with "smoke" in the first line. In the second line, he adds the third rhyme "broke." Instead of two rhymes in two bars, the bars in this song have three rhymes between them.

Eric B. and Rakim's second album was called *Follow the Leader* (1988). After it came out, every rapper was following Rakim's style. Verses became looser and more complex in their rhyming and timing. Before long, some rappers could throw four or five rhyming words into a single bar!

Rakim inspired almost every modern rapper. He paved the way from the simple rapping of Run-D.M.C. to the tricky delivery of later artists such as Nas and Andrē 3000. Listeners still feel the furious force of his rhymes in the rappers he inspired. After splitting with Eric B. in the early nineties, Rakim continues producing his own solo work.

UNUSUAL CHARACTERS AND NEW CREWS

Out of the new school of rap came Richard "Slick Rick" Walters. He was originally from England, and he rapped with a British accent. On-stage, Walters wore an eye patch to cover his blind right eye. His first album, *The Great Adventures of Slick Rick* (1988), established his slippery style. On the track "Children's Story," Slick Rick became a story rapper, someone who tells tales through rhyme. The song showed Slick Rick's gift for mimicry. Rick recruited beatboxer Doug E. Fresh to help with his beats. A beatboxer uses his or her mouth to mimic the sounds of drums and other instruments.

The Juice Crew was a loose collection of characters formed by old-school DJ Marley Marl in the mid-1980s. The Crew included several of Queens's most respected MCs. Big Daddy Kane dropped rhymes at amazing speeds, despite issues with asthma. Kool G. Rap rapped hard-crime stories about growing up in the poor neighborhood of Corona, Queens.

Brooklyn's Boogie Down Productions included KRS-One,

POSSE CUT

The Juice Crew came together on "The Symphony" (1988), released by Marley Marl (RIGHT), It was one of the earliest posse cuts. A posse cut is a rap track on which more than four emcees have verses. "The Symphony" featured all the Juice Crew's key rappers. Big Daddy Kane, Kool G. Rap, Masta Ace, and Craig G. took turns on the mic.

D-Nice, and Scott La Rock. KRS-One (Lawrence Parker) was its leader. He was one of the most committed conscious rappers ever. An admirer of Afrika Bambaataa, KRS-One believed hip-hop lyrics were a force for good in black communities. Producer Scott La Rock was murdered not long after the crew's first album **Criminal Minded** came out in 1987. Though La Rock died young, KRS-One still pays tribute in his rhymes to the talented producer. ★

Slick Rick stood out among other hip-hop artists of the 1980s, because of both his bold image and the British accent in which he rapped.

♪ MUST DOWNLOAD Playlist

BLONDIE
"Rapture" (1980)

SCHOOLLY D
"Gangster Boogie" (1984)

LL COOL J
"I Can't Live Without My Radio" (1985)

RUN-D.M.C.
"King of Rock" (1985)

BEASTIE BOYS
"Rhymin' and Stealin'" (1986)

BOOGIE DOWN PRODUCTIONS
"Dope Beat" (1987)

BIG DADDY KANE
"Ain't No Half-Steppin'" (1988)

ERIC B. AND RAKIM
"Follow the Leader" (1988)

MARLEY MARL
"The Symphony" (1988)

SLICK RICK
"Children's Story" (1989)

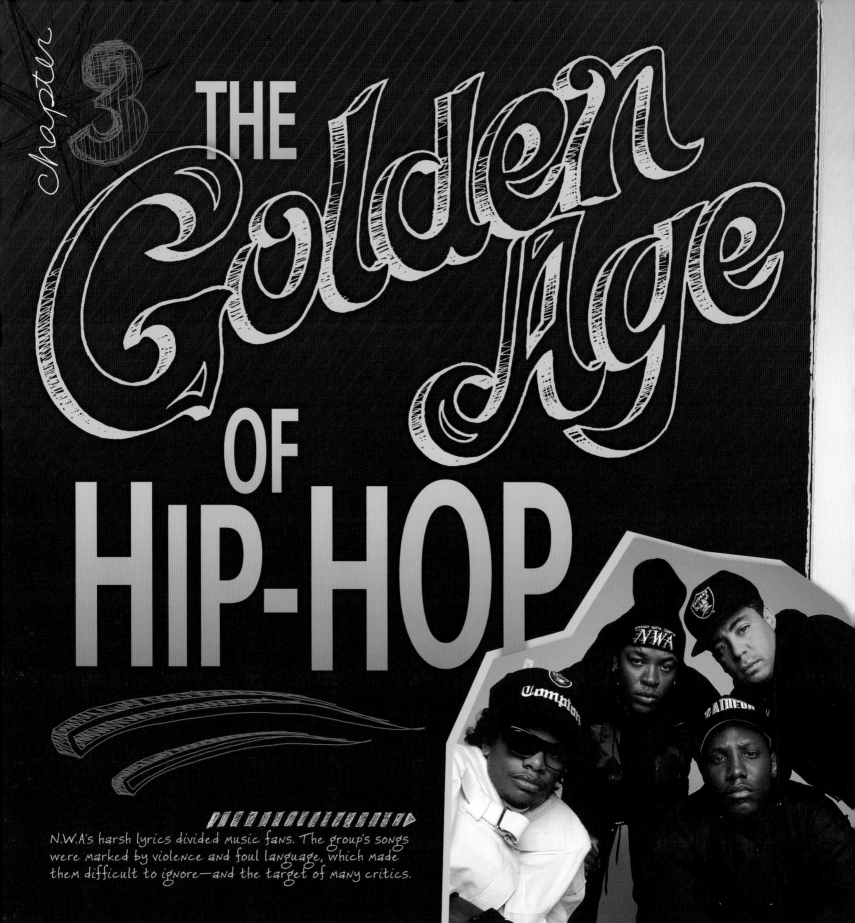

chapter 3

THE Golden Age OF HIP-HOP

N.W.A's harsh lyrics divided music fans. The group's songs were marked by violence and foul language, which made them difficult to ignore—and the target of many critics.

THE GOLDEN AGE OF HIP-HOP WAS A PERIOD OF INTENSE CREATIVITY BETWEEN 1987 AND 1993.

This era launched artists such as De La Soul, Gang Starr, and Public Enemy. Dozens of new groups added new sounds and ideas to the scene.

During the golden age, hip-hop expanded to the West Coast of the United States. The controversial group N.W.A (Niggaz With Attitude) was from Compton, California. Members of the group included rappers Eazy-E, Ice Cube (O'Shea Jackson), Arabian Prince, and MC Ren, producer Dr. Dre, and DJ Yella. N.W.A's West Coast rap was very different from East Coast hip-hop. In time, the music came to be known as gangsta rap for the way it dealt with harsh aspects of street life.

The album **Straight Outta Compton** (1988) was angrier and darker than most rap music at the time. N.W.A's music explored the rage toward the racial discrimination and injustices of white society that many black Americans felt. Some of N.W.A's songs promoted gun violence and rioting in the streets. Other songs used graphic sexual language that was offensive to women. The controversy over the group's explicit, rageful, and often violent language helped N.W.A stay famous. It made celebrities of members Ice Cube, Eazy-E, and Dr. Dre.

The city of Compton, California, was home to the members of N.W.A. It inspired the name of the group's rage-filled debut, **Straight Outta Compton** (1988).

PUBLIC ENEMY BRINGS THE NOISE

Few groups are as important to hip-hop as Public Enemy. Some fans say that its second album, **It Takes a Nation of Millions to Hold Us Back** (1988), is the best rap album ever. Like their idols Run-D.M.C. and the Beastie Boys, the group signed with Def Jam Records. They worked closely with promoter Russell Simmons and producer Rick Rubin.

Public Enemy was famous for its "wall of sound" production style. DJs Terminator X and the Bomb Squad created tracks that were noisy, busy, and packed with samples. Some tracks used car horns or air-raid sirens as part of the beat. The song "Bring the Noise" has more than a dozen different samples playing at once. All of these different parts combine to make beats that sound like nothing else.

Public Enemy had two main rappers: Chuck D (Carlton Douglas Ridenhour) and Flavor Flav (William Drayton Jr.). Chuck D was the leader of the group. Flavor Flav was the hype man. A hype man is a rapping sidekick who gets the audience excited, leading chants and sing-alongs. Together, Chuck and Flav wrote songs criticizing the discriminatory racial policies of the U.S. government, the dangers of drug use, police brutality toward African Americans, and media bias against radical black politics.

The work of civil rights activists such as Martin Luther King Jr. (1929–1968) and Malcolm X (1925–1965) inspired Public Enemy. The group used rap to give a voice to voiceless minorities. For example, Chuck D believed strongly in a proud black culture. In his famous song "Fight the Power," he talks forcefully about creating change and seizing equal treatment. Public Enemy's aggressive attitude—combined with the military-style clothes its members often wore—pushed many listeners out of their comfort zones.

Another member of Public Enemy, Professor Griff, made headlines with controversial remarks about Jews in a 1989 newspaper interview. He claimed Judaism was responsible for "wickedness that goes on around the globe." Chuck D did not support this point of view and kicked Professor Griff out of the group.

SUPERSTARS IN TROUBLE

The golden age was the time of the superstar producer. The Bomb Squad, DJ Premier, Pete Rock, and others created a new style of producing—and some new legal issues. These artists piled sample upon sample while making hip-hop tracks. They didn't always get permission. Sometimes, producers sampled other people's music on new tracks without paying for it. In the early 1990s, the U.S. government created new laws to stop producers from sampling music for free.

The group Public Enemy was revolutionary in more ways than one. Leader Chuck D THIRD FROM RIGHT spat fierce political raps, while Terminator X SECOND FROM LEFT filled tracks with sample upon sample. Chuck, Terminator X, Flavor Flav THIRD FROM RIGHT, and Professor Griff FAR RIGHT are pictured here in 1987 with members of P.E.'s security group S1W (Security of the First World).

After Griff left, Public Enemy continued the fight against racism and oppression—on its own terms. In the song "By the Time I Get to Arizona" (1991), Chuck made threats against the life of the Arizona governor, who did not want his state to celebrate the new federal holiday honoring Martin Luther King Jr. The video for the song aired only once on MTV because of the controversy.

Public Enemy continues to make music that tackles racial injustice, such as in its new album **Most of Our Heroes Don't Appear on a Stamp** (2012). Chuck D is also a respected author and producer. Flavor Flav has appeared on reality shows such as **Flavor of Love** (2006–2008). However, the group is still best known for the sounds of golden age records such as **It Takes a Nation of Millions to Hold Us Back** (1988) and **Fear of a Black Planet** (1990).

Phife Dawg RIGHT and Q-Tip pose for a picture in the early 1990s. Along with producer Ali Shaheed Muhammad, the two emcees formed the core of A Tribe Called Quest.

RHYMES GALORE

While Chuck D was out fighting the power, new rappers were changing the New York sound. The Native Tongues scene was inspired by Afrika Bambaataa's Universal Zulu Nation. With the name "Native Tongues," the groups within this scene honored their African heritage. Members of the Native Tongues crew wore African clothes with tribal designs. Their songs had colorful samples and more upbeat lyrics than the angry social commentators of Public Enemy or N.W.A.

Three smaller groups combined to make Native Tongues: the Jungle Brothers, A Tribe Called Quest, and De La Soul. The Jungle Brothers were some of the first rappers to sample jazz records. On their first album, **Straight Out the Jungle** (1988), the Brothers also sampled house music. This type of electronic dance music was born in Detroit, Michigan, in the 1980s. The Jungle Brothers track "I'll House You" (1988) is called one of the first "hip-house" songs.

A Tribe Called Quest was one of the most famous groups to come out of the Native Tongues scene. Most people can tell a Tribe

song by its slinky, jazzy beats. The emcees Q-Tip and Phife Dawg came on the scene in 1990 with the album **People's Instinctive Travels**. On later albums such as **The Low End Theory** (1991), Tribe even hired established jazz musicians to play on the record. The record still stands out for its horn parts and jazz chord changes.

While Tribe's beats were unique, their slippery flows were what made them legends. Q-Tip and Phife Dawg were so tight as emcees, they could finish each other's rhymes. The group ended its run in the late nineties, occasionally reuniting for live performances. Altogether, they recorded five albums of perfect hip-hop.

Other members of Native Tongues found success in different ways. The rapper Queen Latifah (Dana Owens) broke new ground with her pro-female rap song "Ladies First" (1989). Latifah later became even more famous as an actor in movies such as **Chicago** (2002) and **Valentine's Day** (2010). In addition to winning a Grammy Award for her work in music, Latifah has been nominated for an Emmy and an Academy Award for her work in TV and film.

HIP-HOP
HIPPIES

During the golden age, few groups were as creative as De La Soul. Even the members' names were strange: Trugoy the Dove, Posdnuos, and DJ Pasemaster Mase. Both Trugoy and Posdnuos came up with the names by switching around the letters of their old nicknames. (Trugoy was Yogurt, while Posdnuos was Soundsop.) The group was originally from the suburbs of Long Island, New York. Because its members grew up in the suburbs, their songs had a more upbeat feel than most hip-hop.

Queen Latifah broke into hip-hop alongside other members of New York's Native Tongues scene. She became one of hip-hop's most popular female emcees. She performs here in 1993.

> ## Raps from the suburbs are a little more broad. They don't have the closed-in focus like inner-city raps. In the suburbs you can rap about regular everyday life like going to the park and taking a swim. The rest of America can relate to that.
>
> —Chuck D of the hip-hop group Public Enemy, 1987

De La Soul's first album was titled **3 Feet High and Rising** (1989). It was named after a line in a song by country singer Johnny Cash. Instead of the hardcore beats of Public Enemy and N.W.A, the group sampled bright, positive sounds. De La Soul explained its life motto in the song "The D.A.I.S.Y. Age." "D.A.I.S.Y." was short for "DA Inner Self, Y'all." Because daisies are a type of flower, some people called the group hip-hop hippies. The label stuck, even though they did not think of themselves as hippies (young people known for peaceful protest and unusual dress). For their next album, **De La Soul Is Dead** (1991), the sounds became harsher and less friendly. Even though the group made fun of gangsta rap, **De La Soul Is Dead** was closer to the N.W.A sound than **3 Feet High and Rising**.

INSANE IN THE MEMBRANE

N.W.A was the first group to put California hip-hop on the map. In 1988 the Los Angeles group Cypress Hill brought Latino culture into rap. Rapper B-Real (Louis Reese) led the group. B-Real came from Cuban and Mexican heritage, while the producer Muggs was of Italian and Norwegian descent.

Like N.W.A, Cypress Hill used their songs to diss the Los Angeles police. Songs such as "How I Could Just Kill

De La Soul in 1994, at a concert in New York City. The group's upbeat music gave hip-hop fans an alternative to gangsta rap.

a Man" (1991) protested what the group—like N.W.A and other hip-hop groups before them—believed was the unjust use of violence against people of color by the local police.

Cypress Hill's most famous song is "Insane in the Brain" (1993). In that song, B-Real uses a high-pitched, wobbling rapping style to make it sound as if he is losing his sanity. It became their biggest hit and was even featured on a *Simpsons* episode in 1996. The success of Cypress Hill led to a wave of other Latino artists, such as Big Pun and Fat Joe.

The hip-hop group Cypress Hill, pictured here in the nineties, included members of many different ethnicities. The group's lead rapper B-Real LEFT is one of hip-hop's first famous Latino emcees.

LATINO HIP-HOP

The Cuban rapper Mellow Man Ace (Ulpiano Reyes) was a friend and supporter of Cypress Hill. Ace made hip-hop history himself in 1990. With his Spanglish track "Mentirosa," he scored the first major bilingual (two language) hit in hip-hop. The Puerto Rican rapper Big Pun (Christopher Rios) became the first solo Latino hip-hop artist to sell more than one million albums. Big Pun released his debut album *Capital Punishment* in 1998 and died tragically of a heart failure in 2000.

Like Mellow Man Ace, Immortal Technique (Felipe Coronel) was born outside the United States. He moved from Peru to New York City when he was young. In the early twenty-first century, he began releasing hip-hop albums that criticize racial biases in the music industry and in U.S. government policies. He has many fans, though his controversial songs are not often played on the radio.

The Cuban American rapper Pitbull (Armando Pérez) has taken a different path than radical emcees such as Immortal Technique. His rhymes aim straight for the mainstream. Pitbull was born in Miami, Florida, and made his name by collaborating with the southern rapper Lil Jon in 2002. Pitbull soon started scoring hits of his own, both as a solo artist and with pop stars such as Jennifer Lopez.

NAME WITH AN AIM

"Everybody always asks us why we call ourselves 'niggaz,'" MC Ren said in a 1991 interview, "[but] no matter what you do, everybody's gonna call you that." N.W.A's name, as well as its lyrics, divided African American hip-hop fans. Critics protested the group's use of a term that had been and continues to be a harsh racial insult. The term *nigger* developed in the time of the transatlantic slave trade (1500s–1800s), when Africans were taken captive and sold in North and South America for slave labor. It became an insult used against people of African heritage.

N.W.A argued that "Niggaz With Attitude" was part of the group's take on race relations and inner-city life. N.W.A considered its music "reality rap," and the group's members believed the name reflected the reality of how people outside black culture viewed African Americans. "As long as you remain black, you're still gonna be a nigga," Eazy-E asserted in the same interview.

Arguments about use of the "n-word" in hip-hop do not begin and end with N.W.A. Since the genre began, many fans and artists have insisted that using the word can remove the word's power to hurt. Others have argued that the use of the term should stop completely because of its hateful past. In 2007 Nas announced plans to release an album titled *Nigger*. African American political leaders, including Jesse Jackson and Al Sharpton, who oppose the use of the word protested Nas's decision. In 2008 Nas decided to release the album without a title.

MISCHIEF AND SCI-FI

Meanwhile, alternative hip-hop artists were trying to make music that was different from the hip-hop on the radio. One of the earliest alternative groups was Souls of Mischief. The group came out of the Hieroglyphics crew of Berkeley, California. Souls of Mischief's four young emcees had a hit with the song "'93 Till Infinity" (1993). The song's pleasant, mellow beat brought jazz-rap to the West Coast.

Another member of the Hieroglyphics crew, Del the Funkee Homosapien, would become a legendary alternative rapper. Though he started as a solo artist in the early 1990s, Del became more famous after a collaboration with the pop band Gorillaz. He was a big fan of science fiction and enjoyed rapping about aliens and futuristic societies. Del's album **Deltron 3030** (2000) is about a future world where everyone wants to be a rapper.

Though the golden age of hip-hop ended in the early 1990s, the sounds of those records never went away. Rappers such as Mos Def and Talib Kweli carry on this creative tradition in the twenty-first century. The golden age also helped inspire the indie hip-hop scene. *Indie* is short for "independent"—music that is not recorded for a major label. Many prominent indie rappers, such as Atmosphere, Aesop Rock, and Buck 65, were inspired by early alternative artists. In these ways and others, the legacy of the golden age's music lives on. ★

♪ MUST DOWNLOAD Playlist

N.W.A
"Gangsta Gangsta" (1988)

PUBLIC ENEMY
"Black Steel in the Hour of Chaos" (1988)

BRAND NUBIAN
"Slow Down" (1990)

DE LA SOUL
"A Rollerskating Jam Named 'Saturdays'" (1990)

EPMD FEAT. REDMAN
"Headbanger" (1992)

PETE ROCK AND CL SMOOTH
"They Reminisce Over You" (1992)

A TRIBE CALLED QUEST
"Award Tour" (1993)

CYPRESS HILL
"Insane in the Brain" (1993)

SOULS OF MISCHIEF
"93 Till Infinity" (1993)

GANG STARR
"Code of the Streets" (1994)

DR. OCTAGON
"Blue Flowers" (1996)

chapter **4**

BIGGER *Business,* BIGGER *Beefs*

N.W.A'S STRAIGHT OUTTA COMPTON (1988) WAS THE FIRST SIGN THAT WEST COAST RAP HAD STAYING POWER.

A bitter and violent feud soon broke out between East Coast and West Coast rappers.

At first, the East-West feud inspired the creativity of the golden age. California rappers began saying they could rhyme harder and better than New Yorkers. With so much competition, rappers always had to try out new styles and sounds. But eventually, the feud turned vicious. Disses on records had been friendly and competitive. They became violent and personal. Some of the violence in the lyrics spilled out onto the street. It would cost hip-hop the lives of its brightest talents.

MOST WANTED

Despite its early success, N.W.A had trouble staying together. Ice Cube, the group's main rapper and writer, didn't remain part of the group for long. He left the West Coast in 1989 to make an album in New York. Recorded with Public Enemy's Bomb Squad, **AmeriKKKa's Most Wanted** was Cube's first solo release. The title came from the TV show **America's Most Wanted**, a documentary program about fugitives from justice. The title also made reference to the Ku Klux Klan (KKK), a violent hate group that formed in the 1800s to terrorize blacks and other minorities.

Ice Cube thought of himself as one of "America's Most Wanted" because of his outsider opinions. His album's lyrics were brutal and direct. Cube went after the White House and the Federal Bureau of Investigation for treating people of color unfairly. He also

Ice Cube began his career at the front of N.W.A, but by the start of the nineties, Cube had started releasing popular solo records.

criticized black men who did not resist mainstream white culture.

G-FUNK TAKES THE CHARTS

Ice Cube eventually went back to California to record the classic West Coast albums *Death Certificate* (1991) and *The Predator* (1992). His music started resembling the popular G-funk sound created by N.W.A's producer, Dr. Dre (Andrē Young).

In 1991 Dre was working with N.W.A on their second album *Efil4Zaggin*. It was less successful than N.W.A's first, and the group broke up not long after the album's release. Dre decided to focus on producing records, starting with his solo album *The Chronic* in 1992. *The Chronic* would be the first album released on Death Row Records. Dre and his business partner Marion "Suge" Knight co-owned this new label.

Since Dr. Dre knew he wasn't a very good rapper, he brought in a new emcee named Snoop Dogg (Calvin Broadus). Snoop helped write *The Chronic's* lyrics. He also rapped on almost every track. With new talent on his side, Dre focused on making beats that were funky and catchy. He was inspired by funk legend George Clinton's bands Parliament and Funkadelic, sometimes called P-Funk. Funk is a type of aggressive, groove-heavy music that came out of R & B. G-funk, which stands for "gangsta funk," was like a hip-hop version of Clinton's sound. Dre's song "Let Me Ride" sampled the Parliament track "Mothership Connection (Star Child)" from 1976.

The Chronic ruled the rap charts in 1992. Snoop Dogg became a superstar following the album's huge success. *The Chronic* was followed by Snoop's album *Doggystyle* (1993), another Dre production. Both releases made Death Row Records a major player in the hip-hop business. But as the Notorious B.I.G. would later predict, more money leads to more problems.

TWO TRAGEDIES: TUPAC AND BIGGIE

The Notorious B.I.G. and Tupac Shakur (or 2Pac) were at the center of the East Coast-West Coast rapper feud. Biggie was from Brooklyn, New York. Shakur was a New Yorker who had moved to California in his teen years. At the beginning of the 1990s, the two men were friends. They respected each other as artists and even performed together onstage. By the end of the decade, they were both dead.

Shakur started his career earlier than Biggie. His mother, Afeni Shakur, was a member of the political activist group the Black Panthers. The group fought for civil rights and social justice in the 1970s. Young Tupac was born while she was in jail. He grew up in East Harlem, New York, and later moved to Baltimore, Maryland, before finally settling in Oakland, California.

In Oakland, Shakur got his first rap gig. He started as a dancer and occasional rapper for the group Digital Underground. This led to a record deal and his first album with Interscope Records, *2Pacalypse Now* (1991). The album was inspired by the creativity of the golden age. Some of his lyrics were boastful. But other songs were deeply aware of poverty, drugs, the mistreatment of women, and other issues impacting African Americans.

The album's first single, "Brenda's Got a Baby," tells the story of a twelve-year-old girl who gets pregnant following a sexual assault, has the baby, turns to prostitution to support her child, and is later murdered. In the song, Shakur describes Brenda's tragedy and how it affects her entire community.

Dr. Dre made his name producing albums by N.W.A. He later helped artists such as Snoop Dogg and Eminem reach hip-hop stardom.

Snoop Dogg's laid-back raps were a hit with hip-hop fans who picked up Dr. Dre's album **The Chronic** (1992).

Another track, "If My Homie Calls," was about the friends Shakur left behind in the East, and how they always have a place in his home if they need it.

Meanwhile, the Notorious B.I.G. was making noise on the other side of the country. Biggie Smalls was born Christopher Wallace in Brooklyn. Like many poor black men, he turned to drug dealing to earn a living before making it as a musician. In some of his songs, he describes the pain he felt as a young person with no education and no way off the streets. Biggie was also overweight as a child. Other kids made fun of him because of his large size. This made Wallace more determined to succeed.

Biggie was discovered by a young rap businessperson named Puff Daddy (Sean Combs) in 1992. The next year, the two men formed Bad Boy Records. Biggie's album **Ready to Die** came out on Bad Boy in 1994. With Puff Daddy's guidance, it became a huge success. Some people were calling Biggie the best rapper alive. Nobody could match his delivery or his gift for phrases in songs like "Juicy" and "Gimme the Loot." Just as Shakur came to represent California, Biggie became New York.

Puff Daddy formed Bad Boy Records with Biggie in 1993.

VIOLENCE ERUPTS

In late 1994, Shakur was shot and robbed in the lobby of a New York City recording studio. He survived the attack, but drug use and the media hype surrounding the East-West feud made Shakur suspicious of his former friends. He began to believe Biggie and Combs had set him up. Biggie said that he wasn't involved, but the rivalry was already in full swing. In 1995 Shakur

Tupac Shakur was born on the East Coast, but he became West Coast hip-hop's greatest emcee after moving to California. His raps were sometimes violent and sometimes socially minded, occasionally within the same song.

Biggie Smalls, or the Notorious B.I.G., used hip-hop to escape from the New York City drug trade. He became the face of East Coast hip-hop.

left Interscope to sign with Death Row Records. His song "California Love" (1995) with Dr. Dre brought him into the G-funk community.

At the 1995 Source Awards, a hip-hop award ceremony, the feud got even more personal. Death Row owner Suge Knight criticized Puff Daddy onstage. Meanwhile, both Biggie and Shakur were becoming increasingly paranoid about their safety. Shakur blamed Biggie for the 1994 shooting, although neither Biggie nor Combs was ever charged with involvement in the attack. Shakur also released the diss track "Hit 'Em Up" (1996), which made fun of Bad Boy Records. Biggie was afraid of becoming a target of violence himself.

On September 13, 1996, Shakur was murdered in a Las Vegas, Nevada, drive-by shooting. No one knows who pulled the trigger. Biggie denied having anything to do with it. In fact, Biggie became depressed and more frightened after Shakur's death. Obsessed with being murdered, Biggie recorded one last album, **Life After Death** (1997). In his last days, Biggie expressed sadness about Shakur's death. On March 9, 1997, Biggie was also murdered. As with Shakur, an unknown criminal shot Biggie four times. **Life After Death** came out a few weeks later. No one has been convicted in the shooting of either rapper.

GONE BUT NOT FORGOTTEN

In its short history, hip-hop has felt many losses. Few were more tragic than the death of Jam Master Jay, the original DJ for Run-D.M.C. In 2001 Jason Mizell was shot and killed outside a recording studio in Queens, New York. Police who investigated the crime suspected that the shooter targeted Mizell because of his support for a rapper who had upset a local drug dealer. As of 2012, no one had been convicted of the shooting.

ILLMATIC

Other hip-hop beefs ended on more peaceful terms. The story of Nas and Jay-Z is similar to that of Biggie and 2Pac in many ways. They started with shared respect for each other and later became enemies. For a while, these two powerful emcees battled over the right to be called New York's greatest. But unlike 2Pac and Biggie, Nas and Jay-Z worked out their differences. They understood the death and pain that rap feuds could cause.

Nas (Nasir Jones) was a rapper from Queens who gained respect for his next-level rhyming skills. As a child, he idolized Queens rappers such as Run-D.M.C. and Kool G. Rap. He first appeared on the track "Live at the Barbeque" by the group Main Source. Nas's verse on that track was so strong that he blew away the more famous emcees.

"Live at the Barbeque" led to his first album, *Illmatic* (1994). A hip-hop classic, it combined some of the best beats and rhymes ever produced. Nas could rock the mic in ways that hadn't been heard since Rakim. Tracks such as "N.Y. State of Mind" and "The World Is Yours" were full of genius lines. Only a young rapper and Biggie fan from Brooklyn's Marcy housing projects could compare. His name was Shawn Carter.

TAKING OVER

Carter called himself Jay-Z, after his mentor Jaz-O and New York's J/Z subway line. He became known around New York for his freestyling talents. Early in his career, the unknown Jay-Z beat LL Cool J in a battle rap. His first album, *Reasonable Doubt* (1996), came out a year after *Illmatic*. It signaled a new major talent. After Biggie died, Jay-Z quickly became known as Brooklyn's finest rapper.

The feud with Nas started in 2001. Jay-Z's album from that year—*The Blueprint*—featured the song "Takeover," produced by Kanye West.

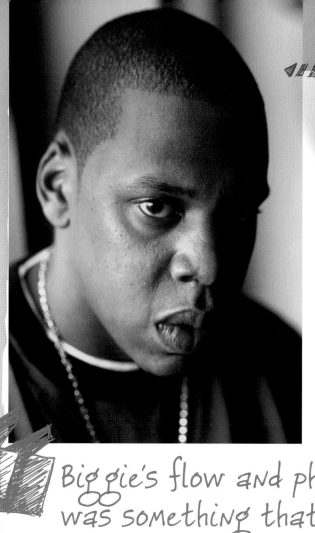

Jay-Z LEFT made his name as a talented freestyle rapper before becoming a global superstar. ON the way to the top, he feuded with fellow New York emcee Nas.

Nas released his full-length debut **Illmatic** in 1994. The album is considered a hip-hop classic.

"Biggie's flow and phrasing was something that had never been done before.... Of the third generation, of the three lyrical kings, Jay-Z is the slickest, Nas is the most cerebral [intellectual], and Biggie is the most explosive."

—Kool Moe Dee, New York rapper, 2003

The Wu-Tang Clan's breakout release, **Enter the Wu-Tang 36 Chambers,** touched on everything from urban violence to martial arts movies. Many of the group's members later became solo stars. Pictured, FROM LEFT, is Ghostface Killah, Masta Killa, Raekwon, RZA, ODB, U-God, GZA, and Method Man. (Not pictured: Inspectah Deck.)

The track seemed to be a diss against Nas. Among other insults, Jay accused Nas of releasing only one good album every ten years. Nas responded with his own diss track, "Ether." The feud was getting dangerous until Kanye West, a fan of both artists, asked the two to make peace. Jay-Z and Nas had both learned the lessons of Tupac and Biggie. They didn't want to see a tragedy like that happen again. By choosing to treat each other with respect, they both continued as successful rap icons. Jay-Z, in particular, is the model of a successful rapper-turned-businessperson.

GANGS OF
SHAOLIN

Although California hip-hop had made it big by the nineties, the New York scene wasn't going away. All across the city, new hip-hop artists were breaking out. A group called the Wu-Tang Clan, from the rough streets of Staten Island, put their borough (which they refer to as Shaolin) on the hip-hop map.

The Clan was a different type of rap group. The huge group featured nine emcees. Members included producer RZA and rappers ODB, Method Man, GZA, Raekwon, and Ghostface Killah. The name "Wu-Tang Clan" came from a martial arts movie. Though they came from unsung Staten Island, their raps were colorful and imaginative. The group's strong performers rapped not only about violence and drugs but also about comic books, chess, and math. The name, "Wu-Tang Clan," was a nod to the group's love of martial arts films.

LAURYN HILL

Hip-hop has traditionally been dominated by men. Though many female emcees have taken up the mic, it is much harder for a female rapper to make it in the industry. It is even rarer for people in the industry to treat female artists with the same respect as male rappers. Lauryn Hill is one of the female emcees who proved that great rapping knows no gender.

Hill was originally part of a rap trio called the Fugees. At the age of thirteen, she began making soulful, intelligent rap songs with emcees Pras and Wyclef Jean. After reaching adulthood, Hill became a solo artist with her blockbuster album *The Miseducation of Lauryn Hill* (1998). The debut won five Grammy Awards including Album of the Year.

Hill has become a somewhat mysterious figure since the release of *Miseducation*. She avoids the press when possible and has not put out another studio album. But she has pursued creative projects in fields such as poetry and has occasionally performed in concert. She has also become the mother of six children. Hip-hop fans, male and female, still hope for a new record.

André 3000 LEFT and Big Boi of OutKast, posing before the MTV Video Music Awards in 2003. Beginning in the nineties, OutKast proved that the South had much to add to hip-hop.

The Wu-Tang Clan's first single was "Protect Ya Neck" (1992). Next was the album **Enter the Wu-Tang 36 Chambers** (1993). It made stars of the whole crew, especially ODB and Method Man. The solo track "Method Man" became a hit for the group, as did "C.R.E.A.M." With the success of **36 Chambers**, RZA also produced beloved classic albums from Raekwon, GZA, and others. ODB died in 2004, but as solo artists and as a group, Wu-Tang Clan continues to give Shaolin a good name.

THE SOUTH GOT SOMETHING TO SAY

The 1995 Source Awards ceremony was best known for feuding between East Coast and West Coast attendees. Even so, a "third coast" made a memorable appearance. While Death Row battled with Bad Boy, an unexpected group won the 1995 award for Best New Artist: OutKast.

As the two members of OutKast made their way onstage to accept the award, the audience showed them no respect. They belonged to neither the East Coast nor the West

Coast. But André 3000 (André Benjamin) and Big Boi (Antwan Patton) knew they deserved the victory. When André gave his acceptance speech, he was booed off the stage after telling the crowd that the South had something to say. Those words predicted the southern rap revolution. Just like N.W.A helped make West Coast rap its own kind of music, OutKast would make the South into its own genre.

Southern rap groups such as UGK and the Geto Boys had released records before André and Big Boi. But OutKast was the first group to take Dr. Dre's G-funk sound and turn it into a "southern thang [thing]." On their first album *Southernplayalisticadillacmusik* (1994), the two emcees shook the world with their bouncy grooves and southern-fried beats. In the next decade, OutKast became one of the most adventurous rap groups ever. Albums such as **ATLiens** (1996) and **Aquemini** (1998) challenged the East-West radio dominance. The albums drew upon traditional blues and country sounds to create music that was uniquely southern. Together with the Atlanta, Georgia, quartet Goodie Mob, OutKast announced the arrival of a new musical coast. ★

MUST DOWNLOAD Playlist

MOBB DEEP
"Shook Ones, Pt. II" (1994)

NAS
"It Ain't Hard to Tell" (1994)

DR. DRE
"Keep Their Heads Ringin'" (1995)

GOODIE MOB
"I Didn't Ask to Come" (1995)

JAY-Z
"Dead Presidents II" (1996)

OUTKAST
"ATLiens" (1996)

2PAC
"To Live & Die in LA" (1996)

UGK FEAT. 3-2
"One Day" (1996)

NOTORIOUS B.I.G.
"Hypnotize" (1997)

WU-TANG CLAN
"Triumph" (1997)

LAURYN HILL
"Doo Wop (That Thing)" (1998)

chapter 5

THE MP3 REVOLUTION

The Internet has changed how hip-hop fans find, share, and listen to music.

THE HIP-HOP WORLD FACED NEW PROBLEMS AT THE END OF THE MILLENNIUM.

So did the rest of the music industry. The popularity of the Internet and a new website called Napster changed the music industry forever. Napster software made it possible for computer users to illegally share and download music over the Internet. Some people in the music industry worried that no one would buy albums anymore. If no one was buying music, producers, rappers, and other musicians could not be paid for their work.

After the music industry took legal action against Napster in 2001—and won—the company shut down. But concerns about illegal downloading did not go away. In the early twenty-first century, fans began to wonder how much it should cost to download a whole song—or if it was OK to share songs online. After all, lending a CD to a friend is not illegal. According to the Napster lawsuit, however, sharing music became stealing when it was done online without paying for the music.

People in the music industry feared that online music theft would ruin the business. In some ways, this turned out to be true. CD sales went down. MP3s (electronic sound files) and MP3 players became the new ways to listen to music. The music industry had to adapt to a new culture where any album could be downloaded digitally. And even though Napster was gone, new websites for accessing music took its place. There was no way to stop people from illegally downloading music.

Yet even with drops in CD sales, the Internet made hip-hop even stronger. Before the year 2000, rappers typically needed the support of major record companies to get played on the radio or on TV. These days, anybody can put a song on YouTube or MySpace. Having an Internet hit is more likely to bring success than getting a video on MTV. Recently, unknown artists have also risen to stardom by using Facebook or Twitter to promote their music. With new voices emerging every day, rap culture in the new millennium is stronger than ever.

> True [hip-hop] empowers people to live an alternative reality— one where they are important and accepted, one where they are productive.
>
> Where they are appreciated, not rejected, for their uniqueness . . .
>
> Our [hip-hop] community is beyond race, religion, and class.
>
> —KRS-One, New York rapper, 2003

THE NEW SUPERSTARS

At the turn of the century, the sounds of the golden age and G-funk gave way to party rap. This style combines hip-hop with modern pop music and R & B. No one was making more epic club music than Dr. Dre. His second album, **2001**, came out in 1999. The dark, menacing beats sounded the future of hip-hop. Dre also produced beats for other rappers. The album introduced the rap mainstream to Dre's new partner Eminem.

One of the biggest party rap hits in 2000 was Nelly's album **Country Grammar**. Nelly (Cornell Haynes Jr.) was born in Texas and grew up in Saint Louis, Missouri. His performances combined rapping and melodic singing. He has a high voice and sometimes wears a bandage on his face onstage and in videos. Songs such as **Country Grammar**'s title track and "Ride Wit Me" helped the album sell 8.4 million copies. Just like in the 1970s, the most profitable rap music was being made for dancing in clubs.

A few years after finding Eminem, Dr. Dre discovered the rapper 50 Cent (Curtis Jackson). He had lived a troubled childhood in South Jamaica, Queens. He began both selling drugs and recording raps in the mid-1990s. In 2000 he was shot nine times, twice in the face, by unidentified attackers. He survived, deciding to pursue a career in hip-hop with renewed energy.

Shortly after recovering from his injuries, 50 Cent grabbed the attention of Eminem, who had heard some of his raps. He started working with Em's mentor Dr. Dre. Together, Dre and 50 made **Get Rich or Die Tryin'** in 2003. Party rap songs such as "In Da Club" were big hits. The slurred rapping style of 50 Cent was no act. It was how he sounded after taking a bullet to the face during his shooting. Like Eminem, 50 also later starred in movies, including **Righteous Kill** (2008) with actors Robert De Niro and Al Pacino. Recently, 50 Cent has become active in African antihunger campaigns.

50 Cent survived a shooting attack in 2000, during which he was shot nine times. He went on to have a string of hit albums in the decade that followed.

EMINEM: TWENTY-FIRST CENTURY SUPERSTAR

Eminem (PICTURED), a white rapper from Detroit, was born Marshall Mathers. **Dr. Dre** and music businessperson **Jimmy Iovine** discovered Eminem after the young rapper won an award in 1997 for freestyling. Eminem and Dre's first album together, *The Slim Shady LP* (1999), featured the breakout hit "My Name Is." That song was one of many where Eminem rapped as his alter ego Slim Shady.

Like **N.W.A**, Eminem was attacked in the media for the violent content of his lyrics, which tackled difficult themes including domestic violence and rape. However, his albums covered a range of subjects. Songs such as "Stan" (2000) explored the dangers of rap fame and Eminem's fear of fans taking his dark, violent lyrics literally. Despite the criticisms, his fan base continued to grow. In 2002

he starred in the movie *8 Mile*, which was based somewhat on his life. The sound track's hit "Lose Yourself" became the first hip-hop song to win the Oscar for Best Original Song.

Eminem laid low for a time following his early success. He did not release a solo album between 2004's *Encore* and 2009's *Relapse*. In between the albums, he sought treatment for a dependence on prescription drugs and coped with the death of friend and fellow rapper **Proof.** Fans were ready for more when Eminem returned. His 2010 album *Recovery* was the best-selling album that year and the best-selling digital album to that point.

THE DIRTY
SOUTH
RISES

Southern hip-hop had achieved mainstream success at the start of the new millennium. Groups such as OutKast in Atlanta and UGK in Houston, Texas, were still going strong. The already successful Out-Kast made a double album in 2003 that broke new ground for southern artists. Instead of working together, Big Boi and André 3000 recorded separate solo albums. Their two-CD release *Speakerboxx/The Love Below* (2003) took over the charts with R & B-influenced songs such as Big Boi's "The Way You Move" and André 3000's "Hey Ya!"

Speakerboxx/The Love Below was the first group hip-hop album to win the Grammy for Album of the Year. With more than ten million CDs sold, it was also one of the last CD block-busters. It came out shortly before people made the switch to down-loading music from online stores.

Producers were as important as rappers to the "Dirty South" sound, as it become known to fans. The West Coast had Dr. Dre. The East Coast had Pete Rock and RZA. The South had Timbaland and the Neptunes. The Atlanta, Georgia, producer Timbaland (Timothy Mosley) began working with R & B singers such as Aaliyah during the 1990s. Mosley soon became known for the beats on rapper Missy Elliot's hits. On hits such as "Get Ur Freak On" (2001), Timbaland and Missy combined smart, club-ready rhymes with R & B grooves and Indian rhythms. Later, Timbaland produced pop albums by Justin Timberlake and Nelly Furtado.

From 2002 onward, there was no escaping the southern twang on hip-hop radio. In Atlanta the producer and rapper Lil Jon created a type of party rap called crunk music. Crunk music features simple keyboard melodies and lots of shouting. Songs such as Lil Jon and the East

THE NEPTUNES

Like Timbaland, the production team the Neptunes also combined elements of R & B and hip-hop. Pharrell Williams and Chad Hugo met as teenagers in Virginia in the late 1980s. Williams and Hugo created their own beats by playing instruments live and then sampling their own parts. Usually, Pharrell played the drums and vocal parts, while Chad played guitar and keyboards.

In the late 1990s, the Neptunes produced records for southern rappers such as N.O.R.E. Since then the Neptunes have produced beats for dozens of rappers and pop stars including Jay-Z and Snoop Dogg. The Neptunes have worked most closely with the Clipse, a gangsta hip-hop duo. The Clipse track "Grindin'" (2002) is a good example of the heavy Neptunes drum sound. When not working with other artists, Hugo and Williams release records as a rock band called N.E.R.D.

Side Boyz's "Get Low" (2002) were easy to dance and sing along to. In New Orleans, Louisiana, the regional form of hip-hop was called "bounce" music. Bounce was inspired by the call-and-response chants of Mardi Gras Indians, native New Orleanians who dress in colorful costumes for the city's Mardi Gras festival. Bounce artists such as David Banner and Three 6 Mafia become known for their songs' ticking beats. In Florida the distorted booms of "Miami Bass" became the sound of up-and-coming rappers such as Rick Ross, especially in Ross jams such as "MC Hammer" and "John (If I Die Today)." In every major city in the South, new hip-hop styles were being born.

FROM BEAT MAKER TO HIT MAKER

Two rappers define recent trends in hip-hop. Their styles are different, but both Lil Wayne and Kanye West overcame hardship on the road to success. Wayne and Kanye also both talked openly about their lives and their emotions. Songs

Missy Elliot's 2001 hit "Get Ur Freak On" was boosted with the beats of famous producer Timbaland.

Kanye West goes hard at New York's Yankee Stadium in 2010. West's music mixes personal confessions with ultra-confident boasting.

such as Wayne's "I Feel Like Dying" (2007) and West's "Hey Mama" (2005) are raw and honest confessions. Fans could relate.

Kanye West grew up in a stable middle-class Chicago household. He loved hip-hop and his mother's old soul records as a child. His mom wanted him to go to college, but he dropped out to work on music full-time. No one thought he would make it. Since he didn't grow up in a low-income area, few people took him seriously as a rapper at first. To break into the business, West became a producer. In 2001 he made some beats for Jay-Z's hip-hop album **The Blueprint**.

On October 23, 2002, West was injured in a car crash. He survived, though his jaw was fractured in several places. Doctors wired his jaw shut so it would heal. This made talking and rapping difficult. Instead of giving up, West turned the story of his injury into a song, "Through the Wire" (2003). He spit verses even while he could barely open his mouth!

West named his first album **The College Dropout** (2004). The album featured a rich, cinematic kind of hip-hop that still sounded classic. At a time when party rap was taking over the radio, the songs were thoughtful, diverse, and full of soulful beats. The track "Jesus Walks" showed West was not afraid to talk about religion or other difficult topics. Other songs, such as "All Falls Down," honored the R & B of his youth.

The College Dropout was Kanye West's first step to stardom. Next, he created his own record label, G.O.O.D. Music. When not writing his own albums, West produced beats for Chicago rappers such as Common and Lupe Fiasco. He also learned to connect with fans by blogging and using Twitter. Even when no one thought he fit the typical hip-hop star mold, West believed in his music. By turning his challenges into songs, he became one of the biggest names in modern hip-hop. West's 2011 collaboration with Jay-Z, **Watch the Throne**, became one of the most downloaded albums in recent music history.

MR. CARTER

Lil Wayne (Dwayne Michael Carter Jr.) spent his teen years in a hip-hop crew known as Hot Boys. He had been hanging around the offices

Lil Wayne got his name because he started young, recording raps in his early teen years. His crew Young Money helps spotlight other up-and-coming rappers.

of the hip-hop record label Cash Money since the age of eleven. He got some attention spitting on tracks with Nelly and the R & B group Destiny's Child. The album **Tha Carter II** (2005) and the track "Fireman" helped him become a well-known solo artist. He boasted of being the best rapper alive. Millions of fans soon agreed.

Lil Wayne has released more music on the Internet than nearly any other rapper. When not working on albums, he makes mixtapes. Mixtapes are collections of songs available on the Internet. On most of his mixtapes, Wayne would take beats from recent R & B and rap hits and add his own vocals. Taking someone else's beat without paying that person is illegal. But mixtape artists avoid legal trouble by offering the music download free. That way, the mixtape artist does not make money from the tape.

Like Kanye West, Wayne is an outspoken figure who has faced personal hardship. In 2005 Hurricane Katrina destroyed parts

of New Orleans, his hometown. Massive storms and flooding killed almost two thousand people and tore apart entire neighborhoods, especially in the poorer areas of the city. One of Wayne's mixtapes, **Dedication 2** (2006), includes a song called "Georgia...Bush." It sampled R & B singer Ray Charles's classic song "Georgia on My Mind" (1960). The song helped Wayne express the anger that African American victims of Katrina felt toward President George W. Bush. Wayne and many others believed that Bush had not directed disaster relief quickly enough or widely enough. This increased the suffering of many people in the disaster area.

Like Kanye West, Wayne is always working with other rappers. He has his own crew, Young Money. Members of that crew include Nicki Minaj, Drake, and New Orleans rapper Curren$y. By working constantly and making free music for his fans, Lil Wayne has become a rap hero for the Internet generation.

Many hip-hop fans heard Nicki Minaj for the first time on tracks by Lil Wayne or Kanye West. But her 2011 album **Pink Friday** proved that Minaj was destined for solo stardom.

HIP-HOP ACROSS THE WORLD

As hip-hop spread around the globe, artists from all over the world have become some of the music's most well-known stars. MC Solaar (Claude M'Barali) (TOP), for example, was born in the African nation of Senegal in 1969. He later moved with his family to Paris, France. He raps in French on top of smooth beats and has worked with American groups such as Gang Starr, De La Soul, and Missy Elliot.

The Haitian rapper Master Dji was an international hip-hop pioneer. In 1982 he recorded the song "Vakans," rapping in Creole, a language spoken in Haiti. Hip-hop was not popular in that country at the time of the song's release, but Haitian hip-hop fans have honored Master Dji's impact in the years since his death in 1994.

The Palestinian group DAM (SECOND FROM TOP) performs mostly in the Arabic language but also in English and Hebrew. DAM songs such as "Born Here" (2004) focus on the conflict between the Middle East's Israeli and Palestinian peoples.

The United Kingdom was late to hip-hop, but Dizzee Rascal (THIRD FROM TOP) helped change that. In the early twenty-first century, his high-pitched raps helped create a type of British hip-hop called grime. The rapper M.I.A. (BOTTOM) was born Mathangi Arulpragasam in England of Sri Lankan heritage. Her music reflects the time she spent in India and Sri Lanka in her youth. M.I.A. songs such as "Boyz" (2007) feature fiery political raps and beats inspired by world music.

RAP INTO THE
FUTURE

Hip-hop started as the music and culture of the streets. DJ Kool Herc and Afrika Bambaataa wanted to show that creativity can win out, even in the toughest environments. Many inner-city kids didn't have money to buy instruments, so they used their voices to make the music they wanted. As the voices grew together, the beats got louder and bigger. In only a few decades, hip-hop has gone from outsider music to a widely popular musical form.

As rapper KRS-One once said, hip-hop is beyond race, religion, or class. It appeals to a wide range of listeners. The Internet has created new ways of listening too. The recent Internet sensation Lil B posted more than one hundred rap songs on YouTube in less than one year. Even Lil Wayne would have a hard time writing that many songs!

With just a few clicks on the computer, anyone reading this book can become a fan of hip-hop. Anyone reading this book can make his or her own hip-hop song. Next time you are on YouTube, try finding an instrumental track or beat that you like. Then start rapping over it. See what happens. Maybe it will sound great, or maybe it will come off as "wack." But with creativity and practice, everyone has the tools to succeed. Are you ready to add your own sounds to the mix? ★

MUST DOWNLOAD Playlist

50 CENT
"Ghetto Qu'ran (Forgive Me)" (1999)

EMINEM
"Lose Yourself" (2002)

MC SOLAAR
"Inch'Alla" (2002)

DIZZEE RASCAL
"Fix Up, Look Sharp" (2003)

KANYE WEST
"Gone" (2005)

YOUNG JEEZY FEAT. AKON
"Soul Survivor" (2005)

CLIPSE
"Mr. Me Too" (2006)

LUPE FIASCO
"Kick, Push" (2006)

T.I.
"What You Know" (2006)

DJ KHALED
"We Takin' Over" (2007)

LIL WAYNE
"I Feel Like Dying" (2007)

UGK FEAT. OUTKAST
"International Players Anthem" (2007)

GLOSSARY

bar: the number of beats it takes for a rapper to speak one line. Most rappers use one or two lines a bar, depending on how faswt they rap.

battle rap: a rap style in which two or more emcees take turns insulting, or "dissing," each other in rhyme form. An emcee wins a battle not only through skilled rhyming but also by having the cleverest jokes and insults.

beat: a measure of rhythm in a song

beatbox: a musical style in which a person makes rhythmic sounds with his or her mouth. Beatboxers use their tongues and lips as instruments.

break: the moment during which a song's groove takes over and the vocals drop out. This part of a song is a "break" from the normal verses and choruses.

conscious: short for "socially conscious." This term describes hip-hop that displays concern for the conditions of a neighborhood or culture as well as encourages justice and self-respect.

DJ: a disc jockey is a musician who uses record albums and a turntable to create new sounds or play breaks for rappers

emcee: the person who delivers rhyming lyrics, or raps, over a song's beats; also called MC

freestyle: to rap without having written down or memorized rhymes beforehand. Freestyling rappers come up with rhymes at the spur of the moment.

mainstream: a collection of widespread trends, or something that is of a culture's most widespread trends

mixtape: a collection of songs that an artist releases separately from an album. While an album will have original beats and production, many mixtapes use beats from other records and hit songs.

posse cut: a single track that features more than four rappers. In most posse cuts, each rapper gets one verse on which to rhyme.

R & B: rhythm and blues is a form of music that originated in the middle of the twentieth century. R & B is danceable music that borrows from African American blues and gospel music traditions.

sample: to take a piece of recorded music from another artist and reuse it as an instrument or part of a beat. Sample is also used to describe the sound that is borrowed for a new song.

scratch: to purposely skip or repeat a record in order to repeat a break or to create a scratchy noise

TIMELINE

1973: DJ Kool Herc hosts his first block party at 1520 Sedgwick Avenue in the Bronx, New York. His style of DJing helps create hip-hop culture.

1979: The Sugarhill Gang releases the first single by a rap group, "Rapper's Delight." It reaches No. 36 on the *Billboard* charts. Kurtis Blow becomes the first rapper to sign to a major record label, Mercury. He also releases the single "Christmas Rappin'."

1981: The Funky Four Plus One perform on *Saturday Night Live*. They are the first rap group to appear on network television.

1983: The group Run-D.M.C. brings in the new school era of hip-hop with its first single "It's Like That."

1984: Russell Simmons and Rick Rubin form Def Jam. The label's first single is T La Rock and Jazzy Jay's "It's Yours."

1986: The rock band Aerosmith appears in the music video for Run-D.M.C.'s version of "Walk This Way." It becomes the first rap video to be played on MTV.

1988: MTV creates its first rap show, *Yo! MTV Raps*.

1995: The East Coast-West Coast hip-hop feud becomes violent when fights between the crews break out at the 1995 Source Awards in New York City.

2000: Dr. Dre is one of the artists to sue Napster, the first software program to allow for illegal online file sharing.

2002: The Detroit rapper Eminem stars in and performs music for the movie *8 Mile*. "Lose Yourself," a hit song from the sound track, is the first rap song to win the Oscar for Best Original Song.

2003: The Atlanta duo OutKast becomes the first hip-hop group to win the Grammy award for Album of the Year.

2004: DJ Danger Mouse releases *The Grey Album*, a combination of beats from Jay-Z's *Black Album* and samples from the Beatles' "White Album" (1968). The release helps create mash-up culture.

2008: Lil Wayne releases *Tha Carter III*, a hit with critics and fans that confirms his status as one of hip-hop's biggest names.

2011: The California rapper Lil B releases an album with the title *I'm Gay*. He is one of the first rappers to criticize homophobic (antigay) lyrics in hip-hop.

2012: At two days old, Jay-Z and Beyonce's daughter Blue Ivy Carter becomes the youngest artist ever featured on the Billboard charts, with the song "Glory."

MINI BIOS

Biggie Smalls (1972–1997): Also known as the Notorious B.I.G., Biggie was the king of New York rap in the 1990s. Together with Puff Daddy, he made Bad Boy Records one of hip-hop's biggest labels. Biggie only released two albums, *Ready to Die* (1994) and *Life After Death* (1997), before being shot to death in 1997.

Kurtis Blow (born 1959): The influential New York emcee Kurtis Blow was the first rapper to sign to a major record label. Blow's song "The Breaks" (1980) was one of the earliest hip-hop hits. In the 1980s, he became a spokesperson against racism and drug use in the hip-hop community.

Chuck D (born 1960): New York rapper Chuck D was the leading voice behind the political rap of Public Enemy. He became one of hip-hop's greatest critics of white authority. Chuck is not only a rapper but also an important activist and hip-hop intellectual.

Dr. Dre (born 1965): Originally a club DJ, Compton, California, native Dre changed West Coast hip-hop with his group N.W.A. He later became one of the most sought-after rapper-producers. As a producer, he discovered artists such as Snoop Dogg, Eminem, 50 Cent, and the Game.

Eminem (born 1972): Marshall Mathers began rapping as a teenager in Detroit, Michigan. He became famous for the sometimes crude, sometimes confessional verses heard on albums such as *The Marshall Mathers LP* (2000). Eminem is the top-selling hip-hop artist of the early twenty-first century and one of the top-selling American solo performers of all time.

Lauryn Hill (born 1975): Lauryn Hill joined rap trio the Fugees while attending high school in Maplewood, New Jersey. She scored the 1995 hit "Killing Me Softly" with the group before achieving solo success in 1998. Her album from that year, *The Miseducation of Lauryn Hill*, won five Grammy Awards.

Jay-Z (born 1969): Brooklyn emcee Jay-Z began his career in the late 1980s. He worked with Biggie and beat LL Cool J in a rap battle. He became arguably hip-hop's most successful businessperson. Jay-Z has sold more than 50 million records, and he owns his own clothing lines and record labels.

Queen Latifah (born 1970): The New Jersey emcee Queen Latifah rose out of the Native Tongues hip-hop scene with hits such as "Ladies First" (1989). She recorded her first album, *All Hail the Queen* (1989), at the age of nineteen. Latifah has also found success as an in-demand film and TV performer.

Lil Wayne (born 1982): Originally from New Orleans, Louisiana, Lil Wayne (nicknamed "Weezy") took over hip-hop with his strange delivery and massive head of dreadlocks. Weezy's rap crew Young Money has some of the most famous names in recent hip-hop, including Drake and Nicki Minaj.

Melle Mel (born 1961): The lead rapper in Grandmaster Flash and the Furious Five is from New York City's Bronx borough. Mel became famous for socially aware raps in such songs as "The Message" (1982). He showed that hip-hop could be about something other than partying and having fun.

Tupac Shakur (1971–1996): Before he became a legendary California emcee, the New York City-born Shakur was a supporting member of the group the Digital Underground. His deep, commanding rapping style and his association with Dr. Dre's Death Row Records made him a worldwide celebrity. His beef with East Coast rappers such as Biggie Smalls may have led to Shakur's shooting death in 1996.

HIP-HOP MUST-HAVES

Must-Have Albums

Grandmaster Flash and the Furious Five, *The Message* (1982)

LL Cool J, *Radio* (1985)

Boogie Down Productions, *Criminal Minded* (1987)

Eric B. and Rakim, *Paid in Full* (1987)

N.W.A, *Straight Outta Compton* (1988)

De La Soul, *3 Feet High and Rising* (1989)

Beastie Boys, *Paul's Boutique* (1989)

Public Enemy, *Fear of a Black Planet* (1990)

Cypress Hill, *Cypress Hill* (1991)

Gang Starr, *Step in the Arena* (1991)

A Tribe Called Quest, *The Low End Theory* (1991)

The Pharcyde, *Bizarre Ride II the Pharcyde* (1992)

Dr. Dre, *The Chronic* (1992)

Wu-Tang Clan, *Enter the Wu-Tang 36 Chambers* (1993)

Nas, *Illmatic* (1994)

Organized Konfusion, *Stress: The Extinction Agenda* (1994)

Pete Rock and CL Smooth, *The Main Ingredient* (1994)

GZA, *Liquid Swords* (1995)

Lauryn Hill, *The Miseducation of Lauryn Hill* (1998)

Deltron 3030, *Deltron 3030* (2000)

T.I., *King* (2006)

Rick Ross, *Teflon Don* (2010)

Big K.R.I.T., *Return of 4Eva* (2011)

Must-Have Songs

Roxanne Shanté, "Roxanne's Revenge" (1984)

Digital Underground, "The Humpty Dance" (1990)

Tupac, "If My Homie Calls" (1990)

Charizma and Peanut Butter Wolf, "Red Light, Green Light" (1991)

Geto Boys, "Mind Playing Tricks on Me" (1991)

Ice Cube, "It Was a Good Day" (1992)

Lords of the Underground, "Chief Rocka" (1992)

Pete Rock and CL Smooth, "T.R.O.Y. (They Reminisce Over You)" (1992)

EPMD Feat. Redman, "Headbanger" (1992)

Souls of Mischief, "'93 Till Infinity" (1993)

Notorious B.I.G., "Gimme the Loot" (1994)

ODB, "Hippa to da Hoppa" (1994)

The Fugees, "Fu-Gee-La" (1996)

UGK Feat. 3-2, "One Day" (1996)

Gang Starr, "Moment of Truth" (1998)

OutKast, "B.O.B." (2000)

Kanye West Feat. Cam'ron and Consequence, "Gone" (2005)

Fat Joe Feat. Lil Wayne, "Make It Rain" (2006)

Big Boi Feat. Gucci Mane, "Shine Blockas" (2009)

Tyler the Creator Feat. Hodgy Beats, "Sandwitches (2011)

Young Jeezy Feat. Freddie Gibbs, "Stripes" (2011)

MAJOR AWARDS

American Music Awards (AMAs): The AMA ceremony is broadcast each year on the ABC television network. TV host Dick Clark created the AMA's in 1973. Unlike the Grammy Awards, the AMAs are awarded based on polls of the public. Nicki Minaj took home the 2011 awards for Favorite Artist and Favorite Album in the Rap/Hip-Hop category.

BET Hip-Hop Awards: This yearly televised ceremony began on the cable channel BET (Black Entertainment Television) in 2006. It focuses solely on hip-hop music. The BET Hip-Hop Awards includes categories such as MVP of the Year, Lyricist of the Year, and DJ of the Year. In 2011 Nicki Minaj won the MVP of the Year award and Lex Luger was honored with Producer of the Year award.

The Grammy Awards: The Grammys are prestigious music awards given yearly since 1959 by the National Academy of Recording Arts and Sciences. Until 1996 the Grammys did not have a Best Rap Album category. The first winner was the group Naughty by Nature for *Poverty's Paradise* (1996). Since then the Grammys have added several additional hip-hop awards. They include Best Rap Song, Best Rap Performance by a Duo or Group, and Best Rap Solo Performance. In 2011 Eminem's *Recovery* received the Grammy for Best Rap Album and Jay-Z's song "Empire State of Mind" won the Best Rap Song award.

MTV Video Music Awards (VMAs): The VMAs, started in 1984, have had an award for Best Rap Video since 1989. DJ Jazzy Jeff and the Fresh Prince were the first group to win for "Parents Just Don't Understand." MTV later replaced the category with the award for Best Hip-Hop Video. In 2011 the young rappers Tyler, the Creator and Nicki Minaj each won an award, for Best New Artist and Best Rap Video, respectively.

NAACP Image Award: Since 1967 the NAACP (National Association for the Advancement of Colored People) Image Awards have honored achievements by people of color in music, film, TV, and literature. Kanye West, Lauryn Hill, and OutKast are all past NAACP Image Award winners.

VH1 Hip-Hop Honors: The cable network VH1's annual ceremony is the hip-hop equivalent of the Rock and Roll Hall of Fame. Instead of giving prizes for best album or best song, VH1 chooses older rap artists and honors their entire careers. Each year about a half dozen rappers and groups are inducted into the Hip-Hop Hall of Fame. Timbaland, Master P, and 2 Live Crew were among those honored in the 2011 ceremony.

SOURCE NOTES

9 Laura Barton, "Rap Is Elitist." Guardian, May 6, 2003, http://www.guardian.co.uk/music/2003/may/07/artsfeatures.popandrock (September 22, 2011).

9 Jim Fricke and Charlie Ahearn, Yes Yes Y'all: The Experience Music Project Oral History of Hip-Hop's First Decade (Cambridge, MA: Da Capo Press, 2002), 43.

16 Russell Simmons and Nelson George, Life and Def: Sex, Drugs, Money and God (New York: Crown Publishers, 2001), 4.

26 Richard Griffin, quoted in Greg Baker, "The Education of Professor Griff," Miami New Times, July 11, 1990, http://www.miaminewtimes.com/1990-07-11/news/the-education-of-professor-griff/ (November 11, 2011).

30 Jeffrey Chang. Can't Stop Won't Stop: A History of the Hip-Hop Generation (New York: St. Martin's Press, 2005), 231.

32 MC Ren, quoted in Matthew McDaniel, "The Controversy Surrounding Their Rise Refuses to Let Up . . . and So Do They," Source, July 1991, http://rapresearcharchive.blogspot.com/2010/06/nwa-interview-in-source-magazine-july.html (November 22, 2011).

32 Eazy-E, quoted in Matthew McDaniel, "The Controversy Surrounding Their Rise Refuses to Let Up . . . and So Do They."

41 Kool Moe Dee, There's a God on the Mic: The True 50 Greatest MCs (New York: Thunder's Mouth Press, 2003), 264.

47 KRS-One, Ruminations (New York: Welcome Rain Publishers), 180–181.

SELECTED BIBLIOGRAPHY

Cepeda, Raquel, ed. And It Don't Stop?: The Best American Hip-Hop Journalism of the Last 25 Years. New York: Faber and Faber, 2004.

Chang, Jeffrey. Can't Stop Won't Stop: A History of the Hip-Hop Generation. New York: St. Martin's Press, 2005.

Charnas, Dan. The Big Payback: The History of the Business of Hip-Hop. New York: New American Library, 2010.

Costello, Mark, and David Foster Wallace. Signifying Rappers: Rap and Race in the Urban Present. New York: Ecco Press, 1990.

Dolnick, Sam. "Hope for a Bronx Tower of Hip-Hop Lore." New York Times. September 6, 2010. http://www.nytimes.com/2010/09/07/nyregion/07sedgwick.html?_r=1&adxnnl=1&ref=nyregion&adxnnlx=1311620861-AqmavLLmX2UtHp+yciyRGw (July 1, 2011).

Fricke, Jim, and Charlie Ahearn. Yes Yes Y'all: The Experience Music Project Oral History of Hip-Hop's First Decade. Cambridge, MA: Da Capo Press, 2002.

George, Nelson. Hip-Hop America. New York: Penguin, 2005.

Green, Tony. "Remembering the Golden Age of Hip-Hop." Msnbc.com, August 2, 2004. http://today.msnbc.msn.com/id/5430999/ns/today-entertainment/t/remembering-golden-age-hip-hop/ (July 1, 2011).

Hess, Mickey, ed. Hip-Hop in America: A Regional Guide. Santa Barbara, CA: Greenwood Press, 2010.

Independance. "Hip-Hop, the History." Independance, 2006. http://www.independance.co.uk/hhc_history.htm (August 1, 2011).

McFarland, Pancho. Chicano Rap: Gender and Violence in the Postindustrial Barrio. Austin: University of Texas Press, 2008.

McLeod, Kembrew. "How Copyright Law Changed Hip-Hop." AlterNet, June 1, 2004. http://www.alternet.org/story/18830/ (July 1, 2011).

McQuillar, Tayannah Lee. When Rap Music Had a Conscience: The Artists, Organizations, and Historic Events That Inspired and Influenced the Golden Age of Hip-Hop from 1987 to 1996. New York: Thunder's Mouth Press, 2007.

Sarig, Roni. Third Coast: OutKast, Timbaland, and How Hip-Hop Became a Southern Thing. Cambridge, MA: Da Capo Press, 2007.

Schloss, Joseph G. Making Beats: The Art of Sample-Based Hip-Hop. Middletown, CT: Wesleyan University Press, 2004.

LERNER

EXPAND LEARNING BEYOND THE PRINTED BOOK. Download free, complementary educational resources for this book from our website, www.lerneresource.com.

SOURCE™

FURTHER READING, WEBSITES, AND FILMS

Allen, Amy Ruth. *Queen Latifah: From Jersey Girl to Superstar.* Twenty-First Century Books: Minneapolis, 2012.
This title explores the art form of graffiti and the culture that surrounds it.

Find out more about Queen Latifah, one of hip-hop's pioneering female rappers—and one of its biggest crossover stars. This book follows Latifah as she made the jump from the Native Tongues scene to award-winning films and television.

Anniss, Matt, and Lisa Regan. *Being a DJ.* Lerner Publications: Minneapolis, 2012.
This title looks at what it's like to be a professional DJ. The book features internationally acclaimed DJs such as David Guetta, Felix Da Housecat, and The Chemical Brothers, as well as turntablists such as Grandmaster Flash. It covers music genres from house, techno, and drum and bass to hip-hop, reggae, and dubstep.

Bradley, Adam, and Andrew DuBois, eds. *The Anthology of Rap.* New Haven, CT: Yale University Press, 2010.
This eight-hundred-page anthology is the first major collection of hip-hop lyrics to see print. Included lyrics cover the history of hip-hop, from Afrika Bambaataa to Young Jeezy.

Buckholz, William. *Understand Rap: Explanations of Confusing Rap Lyrics You and Your Grandma Can Understand.* New York: Abrams Image, 2010.
This humorous book picks out lines from rap songs and attempts to explain what they mean with as much detail as possible. By exploring the meaning behind some of these lines, hip-hop fans can learn a lot about what certain slang terms mean.

Copyright Criminals. Directed and produced by Benjamin Franzen and Kembrew McLeod. New York: Indiepix Films, 2010.
This PBS documentary covers the history of sampling in hip-hop, focusing on the laws and rights of samplers and producers. The documentary also includes video footage of hip-hop DJs showing off their techniques.

Giovanni, Nikki, ed. *Hip-Hop Speaks to Children with CD: A Celebration of Poetry with a Beat.* Naperville, IL: Sourcebooks Jabberwocky, 2008.
Giovanni's book brings African American and hip-hop history together. Fans of words and language will enjoy the book's balance between rap lyrics and speeches from Martin Luther King Jr. and Frederick Douglass.

Gogerly, Liz. *Graffiti Culture.* Lerner Publications: Minneapolis, 2012.
This title explores the art form of graffiti and the culture that surrounds it.

Golus, Carrie. *Russell Simmons: From Def Jam to Super Rich.* Twenty-First Century Books: Minneapolis, 2012.
Find out more about the founding of Def Jam Records. By following the life of hip-hop businessperson Russell Simmons, Golus explains how rap music became big business.

———*Tupac Shakur: Hip-Hop Idol.* Minneapolis: Twenty-First Century Books, 2010.
This book follows the life of Tupac Shakur from the years before he was 2Pac, growing up in New York City and Baltimore, Maryland, to his rise to hip-hop stardom on the West Coast. It also explores the East Coast–West Coast feud and the impact of Shakur's death on hip-hop culture.

Jay-Z. *Decoded.* New York: Spiegel & Grau, 2010.
The rapper's first book is part memoir, part tribute to hip-hop. Fans of Jay-Z will enjoy this book's autobiographical sections, which describe his journey to fame. Other parts of the book focus more on other rappers Jay-Z admires and their techniques.

Lazerine, Cameron, and Devin Lazerine. *Rap-Up: The Ultimate Guide to Hip-Hop and R&B.* New York: Grand Central Publishing, 2008.
For readers interested in a longer and more detailed history, this book covers nearly all the major figures in hip-hop and R & B. The book also includes multiple-choice trivia questions in every chapter and a section that covers hip-hop films.

"What Hip-Hop Means to Me."
http://solomoncomissiong.com/aboutus.aspx
Solomon Comissiong is an educational consultant and activist. Comissiong sees hip-hop culture as a tool to motivate. The essay on his website, "What Hip-Hop Means to Me," is a great introduction for readers interested in hip-hop and social justice.

INDEX

ABOUT THE AUTHOR

Nathan Sacks is a student, writer, and music fan born and raised in Ames, Iowa. He currently lives in Queens, New York, where he is studying for a master's degree in English. In his spare time, he enjoys reading, playing guitar, movies, hanging with his rebel-cat Uzi, and writing. His favorite rap groups include the Wu-Tang Clan, OutKast, and Gang Starr.

PHOTO ACKNOWLEDGMENTS

The images in this book are used with the permission of: © Pavel Chernobrivets/Dreamstime.com, pp. 1, 2, 4; © iStockphoto.com/Aleksandar Petrovic, p. 3; © Tom Cunningham/NY Daily News Archive/Getty Images, p. 5 (left); © Anthony Barboza/Archive Photos/Getty Images, p. 5 (right); © Leo Vals/Hulton Archive/Getty Images, p. 6; © Ted Thai/Time & Life Pictures/Getty Images, p. 7 (top); © Paul Giamou/Workbook Stock/Getty Images, p. 7 (bottom); © David Corio/Michael Ochs Archives/Getty Images, pp. 8 (top), 13 (top), 21, 27; © Tim Hall/Redferns/Getty Images, p. 8 (bottom); © Soul Brother/FilmMagic/Getty Images, p. 9; © Kevin Mazur/WireImage/Getty Images, p. 10; © Peter Noble/Redferns/Getty Images, p. 11; ITV/Rex USA, p. 12; © iStockphoto.com/hudiemm, pp. 13 (bottom), 23 (right), 33, 45, 55, 57, 59, 61, 63; © Lynn Goldsmith/CORBIS, pp. 14, 24; © Frank Edwards/Archive Photos/Getty Images, p. 15; © Michael Grecco/Hulton Archive/Getty Images, p. 16; © Ebet Roberts/Redferns/Getty Images, p. 17; © Neal Preston/CORBIS, pp. 18, 37 (left); © Michael Ochs Archives/Getty Images, pp. 19 (top), 20, 22; © Denise Truscello/WireImage/Getty Images, p. 19 (middle); © Al Pereira/Michael Ochs Archives/Getty Images, pp. 19 (bottom), 23 (left), 41 (both); David Leeson/KRT/Newscom, p. 25; © Chris Carroll/CORBIS, pp. 28, 35; © Tim Mosenfelder/Getty Images, p. 29; © David Corio/Redferns/Getty Images, p. 30; © Robert Knight Archive/Redferns/Getty Images, p. 31; © KMazur/WireImage/Getty Images, pp. 37 (right), 51 (top); © SGranitz/WireImage/Getty Images, p. 38 (left); © Ron Galella/WireImage/Getty Images, p. 38 (right); © Des Willie/Redferns/Getty Images, p. 39; © Bob Berg/Getty Images, p. 42; © Jeremy Bembaron/Sygma/CORBIS, p. 43; AP Photo/Mary Altaffer, p. 44; © Jim Craigmyle/First Light/Getty Images, p. 46; © Eamonn McCabe/Redferns/Getty Images, p. 48; © Chad Batka/CORBIS, p. 49; © Carlo Allegri/Getty Images, p. 50; AP Photo/Jason DeCrow, p. 51 (bottom); © Kevin Winter/Getty Images, p. 52; © Chelsea Lauren/WireImage/Getty Images, p. 53; © Bertrand Guay/AFP/Getty Images, p. 54 (top); © Brian Ach/WireImage/Getty Images, p. 54 (second from top); © CFlanigan/FilmMagic/Getty Images, p. 54 (second from bottom); © John Shearer/WireImage/Getty Images, p. 54 (bottom).

Front cover: © Beto Hacker/The Image Bank/Getty Images.
Back cover: © iStockphoto.com/hudiemm.

Main body text set in Arta Std Book 12/14
Typeface provided by International Typeface Corp